I0111975

Ramblin' with Ralph

Ralph Sproles

Ramblin' with Ralph

copyright © 2024 Ralph Sproles
ISBN: 978-1-959700-42-5

Contents

DEDICATION

I wish to dedicate this book first to my wonderful Lord, who started me on this rewarding journey and has faithfully been with me every step of the way.

Secondly to my faithful wife, Ricki, who stood by me on this spiritual adventure. What a blessing she has been.

Also, to my family, some who are already in their heavenly home and some who are still running the race with me, whom I dearly love.

And finally, to my host of Christian friends who have made my earthly journey unbelievably exciting and enjoyable.

Thank you and may the Lord bless you,
Ralph

ACKNOWLEDGMENTS

I am deeply indebted to my friends for their willingness to assist me through the process of publishing my first book:

Arden Browder

Keith Hale

Judy Slate

Steven Smith

Chad Tucker

INTRODUCTION

I have known Ralph Sproles for seventy years. He is a great preacher and a wonderful friend, greatly loved by the thousands of people who have heard him in churches where he has served as pastor and in the large number of congregations where he has held revivals.

He graduated from Johnson Bible College, now Johnson University, and served on the Board of Trustees for twenty-four years and was Chair of the Board of Trustees for twenty years. Ralph is a model product of Johnson's mission, to educate students to expand the Kingdom of God.

The reason he has been so effective in his preaching is because his sermons are Biblical, practical, and life changing. Ralph is a master storyteller, filling his messages with attention getting illustrations, some humorous and others serious. You will easily recognize these qualities and laugh and cry with him as you read.

Dr. David Eubanks
President Emeritus of Johnson University

A personal message from Dr. Davey Stallings, MD:

Ralph, we met in early 1961when you came to the office as a patient, soon after I came to Rural Hall. It did not take long for us to become good friends. I have shared a lot of your "rambling" with you over these sixty-four years through keeping you company at revivals, bus tours, family vacations, etc. Thanks for surprising me with your talent as an author to share some of your ramblings with your many old friends and using this book to make new friends. You show that Christians can enjoy a smile and even a good belly laugh. Best wishes to a true best friend.

PROLOGUE
My Call to the Ministry

I once knew a very witty fellow who had a secular job then he started preaching. One day he asked me if I was called to preach. I told him, "Yes." He said, "I was too. I got up one morning craving chicken and did not want to go to work." I got a laugh out of that.

My call to the ministry was not that light-hearted. It was both emotional and convicting. In 1953, I graduated from high school with no goals in life. I was working full time at Acme Super Market. America still had the draft to recruit young men for service. I figured it would not be long before Uncle Sam would say, "Boy, I want you!"

My mom knew one Sunday evening after I came home from church I was upset. She started questioning me to find out what was bothering me. "Did something happen at church tonight?" "No ma'am." "Are you having problems at work?" "No ma'am." "Are you having girlfriend problems?" "No ma'am." At this point I went upstairs to my room. I thought by morning I would have slept it off.

God and I wrestled, kin to Jacob's (Genesis 32:22-30), until around two or three in the morning. I finally said to Him, "God, I don't know why you are troubling me so, but if you want me to go to Johnson Bible College, I'm ready." And I fell off to sleep. I recall the next morning as if it were yesterday. I said, "Mom, do you think it is still possible for me to go to Johnson and be a preacher?" Mom began to cry because she had been praying for this. She said, "I will scrub floors if I have to to see that you go." I finally found direction and purpose for my life. I have never questioned one time if I am fulfilling God's will for my life!!

My favorite verse of scripture is I Timothy 1:12 (KJV), "I thank Christ Jesus our Lord, who hath enabled me, for that He counted me faithful, putting me into the ministry." The Apostle Paul expresses my thoughts and feelings better than I can.

Like Paul, I never felt I chose to be a minister, but God placed me in the ministry.

Ramblin' Through My Story

My Story

It all began in Bluefield, West Virginia, on January 3, 1936, the day I was born to Raymond and Della Sproles. Mom was a homemaker and the family anchor. Dad worked at various jobs to provide well for his family of six: Mom, Dad, Betty, Bob, Brenda, and me. He was a truck driver, bus driver, auto mechanic, and in emergency medical services. He was gifted and a "jack of all trades." Because I never took an interest in the things my dad did, he told a family friend, "Ralph will never amount to anything." I learned about this at my parents' Golden Wedding Anniversary. I never did muster up enough nerve to ask my father if he had changed his mind. I hope he did.

We lived close enough to the schools, elementary through high school, that I could walk. I graduated from Beaver High School in 1953.

In my growing up years we lived three blocks from Grace Methodist Church. Our mother took us to church every Sunday. Dad did not go with us. I recall going to the Methodist church camp one summer. Because I was small, the campers called me "peanut." I'm glad that nickname didn't stick. I was baptized (sprinkled) at the Methodist church.

I Told a "Story"

When I was five years old, we lived in Princeton, West Virginia. On a pretty and sunny summer afternoon, my mother had laid down to rest. A fellow came by with a black and white pony. He also had a tripod camera. He asked me if I wanted my picture taken sitting on the pony. "Of course," I said, "let me ask my mother." I asked my mother, and she said, "No." Being a city boy who had never been around any animals bigger than a cat or dog, I told the man it was okay. I did not know what kind of punishment I was going to get for disobeying my mother but thought it would be worth it to get on that pony.

When mother did not see me for a while, she came looking for me. There I was smiling sitting on the pony looking like, I thought, a young Roy Rogers.

I do not think I have ever asked Jesus to forgive me for telling that lie. If I did not it is never too late. Please forgive me Lord! (I still have a couple of pictures sitting on the pony along with a childhood memory.)

Ralph at five-years-old on a pony

Close Call with Death

In my younger years, our family would go on vacation to Norfolk, Virginia, staying with a family who rented cottages on the beach. During one of these trips to the beach when I was around seven or eight years old, I went walking alone on the beach. I could not swim – still cannot. I was walking in water no higher than my knees. Suddenly, I am in water over my head. Naturally, I panicked. When I came up, I screamed for help, but nobody came to my rescue. I went under the water several times. Suddenly, a wave pushed me towards the beach getting me on solid ground.

After that scary ordeal, someone explained to us later that an amphibious boat which they used to transport soldiers during World War II had been in that area. When it reversed its engine to go back into the ocean, it made a big hole in the sand. This is what I had stepped into while walking in the water. In later years, I came to realize God saved me for a purpose. I have tried to find and fulfill that purpose.

My First Job

In my first paying job, I earned one dollar a day working at Gott's Pharmacy. It was two blocks from our house in Bluefield, West Virginia. My two responsibilities were delivering prescriptions by bicycle and working the soda fountain. In those days, you were called "soda jerks." If the customer did not appreciate your job performance, they would just call you "a jerk." Being only fifteen, I had to get a work permit from the employment office. Years later, I told the people at Poplar Springs, "If you do not think I have come a long way, my first job was 'peddling drugs' and now here I am your preacher." Did you get the pun—bicycle and peddling?"

Ralph Liked to Party

My mother was asked to describe her children. She described each one: my older sister Betty, my younger brother Bob, and my baby sister Brenda. Then my mother was asked, "What about Ralph?" She replied, "Ralph liked to party." She was right.

I worked at Acme Supermarket in Bluefield on the weekends and in the summer. I kept a running charge account at a local men's clothing store. I bought a white dinner jacket, black tuxedo pants, maroon bow tie, boutonniere, and oh, yes, I even had the Elvis Presley "blue suede shoes." When someone said, "Let's party," I was, of course, dressed and ready to go.

Ralph in his white jacket

Tragic Death of My Friend

In the spring of 1953, I was getting ready to graduate from Beaver High School in Bluefield, West Virginia. Our school choir planned a trip to Pinnacle Rock State Park as a final get together before graduation. We had a fun time that day with our friends, until the drive home.

Just before dusk, a horrible accident occurred. Jimmy, my friend, was sixteen and finishing his freshman year. I was riding in a pickup truck in the front seat with Bob, the driver, and his girlfriend. Jimmy, his girlfriend, and two other girls were riding in the back of the truck. Jimmy did not want to sit beside his girlfriend because they had a "sweetheart spat" that afternoon, so he stood up against the truck cab. The road was curvy, and Jimmy suddenly lost his balance. He tried to grab the side of the truck, but the centrifugal force threw him under the left rear wheel running over his head. The girls screamed. Bob, in a state of hysteria turned around, driving back to the scene of the accident. Because of the sloped curve, Jimmy's blood had already crossed the highway. We tried to get someone to stop to help us. Finally, someone stopped. They transported Jimmy to the hospital in Bluefield. He was declared dead.

For the next few months, sleep was almost impossible. I would visualize that scene over and over, hearing the wheel rolling over Jimmy's head. It was inescapable. I hope Jimmy was spiritually prepared. Death can come to us quickly and unexpectedly. I knew I was not prepared.

That experience impacted me greatly as I was searching for direction in my life. This unforeseen and horrible accident made me realize how fragile life really is.

A North Carolina Visitor

When I was still in high school with no plans to go to college, I honestly had no plans for my life. I enjoyed church so I would pass out bulletins and talk to people before and after church. There was a maiden lady from King, North Carolina, who came to our church in West Virginia to visit two maiden ladies who were college school mates of hers. (She told me this story years later.) She told her friends, "That young man needs to be a preacher." She must have known something I did not know. About six or seven years later, Ricki and I came to Poplar Springs. Guess what, she was the organist at the church. I was her preacher until she went to be with the Lord. What a small world. My, how God works!

The Three Biggest Spiritual Influences in My Life

I once read when you see a turtle on a fence you know someone helped it get there. I am eternally indebted to these spiritual influences in my early life:

My Mom –

We lived at 604 3rd Street in Bluefield, West Virginia, three blocks from Grace Methodist Church. My father did not go with us.

In my junior year at Beaver High School, my parents found a little white cottage with three acres of land in Green Valley between Bluefield and Princeton. To buy the house, they needed to sell the house we lived in. Our house was on the market for what seemed like forever. Mom and Dad were discouraged, and Dad said, "Let's just take the sign down and forget it." Mom said, "Let me pray one more day." That afternoon a couple came by, saw the sign, and the wheels started turning. We got the house in Green Valley. I was not happy about moving and leaving my friends, but God was leading our whole family in a different direction. We made a one hundred and eighty degree turn toward the Lord, hallelujah! It did not happen overnight. It's always in God's timing and He is patient.

I authored this poem in 1954 which sheds a little light on my struggles during my teen years...

Christ forgives but I did not know that the way of the cross leads home.

So, over this worldly life I went in dark black sin to roam.

Christ called to me one day and said, "Follow me, my Friend."

But I answered, "No, not now, but you may try again."

He said, "But, my boy, you are lost from God's wonderful Holy Land.

But meekly I replied, "I'll stay with this worldly band."

And when I thought no more of this man in the skies above,

He spoke to me again once more and told of His undying love.

This time I responded to His compassionate love and answered His last call.

Now over my life, He has taken the lead, and I've crowned Him 'Lord of all.'

My Preacher– Harold Noe

We started attending Calfee Memorial Christian Church. The preacher was a young single man still attending Johnson Bible College. He was gifted and dedicated to the Lord's work. He would stand in the pulpit each Sunday with his open Bible and preach.

He occasionally came to our house with cheese and bread for Mom to fix toasted cheese sandwiches for lunch. Afterwards, we would go out to the yard and play ball. I began to get a whole new image of preachers — they were normal people who enjoyed the same things I did.

Harold Noe (left) and Ralph

Johnson Bible College--

On April 5, 1953, my father, my younger brother, and I were baptized by Preacher Harold. What an influence he had on my family and me. He also baptized Ricki's family. Harold encouraged me to go to Johnson Bible College now known as Johnson University.

When I enrolled in college in the fall of 1954, I was not prepared for college life. I had never intended to go to college, so I struggled academically. I loved this place in the foothills of the Great Smokey Mountains.

I had great professors and made life-long friends which grew me tremendously. They all accepted and encouraged the mountain boy from West Virginia. I sang in the choir and was part of a quartet, The Watchman. In my later years, I served twenty-four years on the Board of Trustees and as chairperson for twenty years. What a delightful experience serving with several of God's finest servants. This was one of the highest honors of my life. These people were businessmen, women, and preachers. We were a team serving along with the stellar leadership of Dr. David Eubanks and his model hostess wife Margaret. Who can forget her special Baked Alaska dessert?

Ricki and I have financially supported Johnson since I graduated. I will not live long enough to repay the debt I owe Johnson Bible College. To God Be the Glory.

Ralph and Firecrackers

When I was around ten years old living in Bluefield, I went up the street to visit my friend. We decided it would be a clever idea to set off a few firecrackers knowing this was against the city ordinance. A "nice" neighbor called the police. The police officers came to my home. Of course, my mom knew nothing about what we had done. The officers told her to tell me not to do that anymore. Mom asked my brother-in-law to give me a little talk about obeying the law. Okay, I got it.

Two or three weeks later, the police pulled my brother-in-law over for throwing a firecracker out of his car window. I did not learn about this incident until sometime later. As the old saying goes, "You need to practice what you preach!"

At Johnson Bible College (now Johnson University), the undergraduates always had final exams the week after the seniors graduated. Everybody was anxious and nervous. One evening, a classmate and I decided it would be a fun idea to set off firecrackers in the boy's dormitory. Afterwards, one of the other students came to my room and told me that Mr. Clark, Academic Dean of Johnson, is going door to door to find out who set off the firecrackers. I thought he was kidding me, so I walked out of my room into the hall. To my surprise, there was Dean Clark. He spoke to me but did not say anything about firecrackers.

I told my "partner in crime" the next morning we needed to go to his office and admit it was us. We did. We were nervous. Dean Clark was a good man, but a very stern man. He looked at me and said, "Ralph, I didn't think you would do something like that." I felt lower than a snake's belly. For our punishment, we had to stand up during lunch in the cafeteria and apologize to the student body for the disturbance we made in the boy's dorm.

My friend said, "I want to apologize for some of the noise in the boy's dorm last night." I stood up and said, "I want to apologize for the rest of it." Everybody laughed, even Dean Clark with his distinctive laugh.

One of My Dating Experiences

I dated Ricki's older sister Wanda known as "Babe" a few times before I dated her. After Ricki and I got married, she said, "Ralph, I looked out the window and watched you kiss Babe good night. I said, "You must have liked what you saw." I told her I was only waiting around for her to grow up. After all, there is a big difference between thirteen years old and eighteen years old. They would have put me in jail. After a few years, the age difference did not matter now that we are eighty-three and eighty-eight.

Another Close Call with Death

Between my freshman and sophomore years of college (1955), I preached my first two revivals. The second was at a small church in Montcalm, West Virginia, near Bluefield, West Virginia. A friend of mine who was enrolling in Johnson Bible College that fall was leading the singing. We were on our way to Montcalm on a two-lane road going uphill. George was driving his car perhaps a little fast. He was trying to pass a fully loaded slow moving dump truck. Just as he started, he saw a car coming down the hill in our passing lane. He slammed on the brakes but had none. With nowhere to go, he shot across that lane and hit the guard rails between the car and going over the hill. We had just avoided a head-on collision. Once again, I realized that was the hand of our Good Shepherd.

As I matured and looked back upon two close calls with death, I realized "only one life will soon be past, only what has been done for Christ will last."

My First Revival

In the summer of 1955, I preached my first revival in a Methodist Church at a coal mining camp called Piedmont, West Virginia. This was the first of two hundred and fifty in my seventy years in the ministry. The church had been a one-room schoolhouse that was converted and heated with a potbelly stove.

How did this happen? I was preaching at the Christian Church in Matoka, West Virginia, while their preacher was recovering from a heart attack. The preacher at the local Methodist Church in town approached me and asked if I would like to preach a two-week revival at the church where he conducted services two Sunday nights a month. For a nineteen-year-old boy who wanted to be preacher, it was like saying 'sick 'em to a dog.' I had only attended college one year; I did not have one sermon prepared, much less fourteen. Oh, what those poor people had to listen to! When you jump in before you think, you learn to sink or swim.

I told the preacher, "Yes, under one condition: that anyone who accepted the Lord, we would immerse them." He replied,

"That is no problem." In the meeting, he and I baptized eighteen people in a pond on Sunday afternoon.

One baptism in the revival I remember distinctly. Two sisters in their early twenties wanted to be baptized together. Wearing white dresses, made by their mother, with gravel sewed in the hems so they would not float. The sisters locked arms, and we baptized them simultaneously. You do not forget moments like that.

Ralph (left) baptizing at first revival in 1955

Don't Forget to Communicate

Another memorable experience about my first revival. The music leader George and I stayed in the parsonage with the preacher and his wife. They were a sweet elderly couple with a gracious spirit. They lived in a two-story white house with a back porch covered with a tin roof. More about this later.

The preacher told us they would feed us breakfast each morning. During the day while visiting the mining community, some of the ladies of the church would provide us with the other meals. On the first day, we visited people in the community and led the church service in the evening. No one fed us and we had little money. This was before McDonalds or Pizza Hut.

When we arrived back at the preacher's house that evening, we noticed a large apple tree in the backyard. At this point, we were ready to eat anything. It was a moonlit summer night so six foot three George climbed onto the porch roof in his "tighty whitie" undershorts to get us a few apples. Almost seventy years later I can still see George in his underwear gathering apples.

The next morning the preacher asked, "Who did you eat with yesterday?" I looked at George and George looked at me. Neither of us wanted to answer him. We didn't want him to be embarrassed. We finally said, "No one."

I don't need to tell you during the remainder of the revival (two weeks) we ate well---VERY WELL!

The ministry can provide you with so many memories. You could write a book --- which I am doing.

What If?

When I was in college my grandmother whom we called "Sprolesie" moved in with us after my grandfather died.

Nineteen fifty-seven, the summer before I was to return to Johnson Bible College for my senior year, my mother and father told me they did not have the money for me to go back to school. My mom and dad sacrificed greatly to send me to college. I appreciate that more now than I did then. Age has a way of putting things in a truer perspective.

Sometime later Sprolesie called me into her room. I think she had been talking with my mother. She told me that she had received insurance money when my grandfather died. She wanted to give me the tithe from the policy for me to go back to school. It was three hundred dollars. That was a sizable amount of money in 1957.

I have often wondered "What If" Sprolesie had not given me the money. I may not have returned to college. My life could have gone in a totally different direction.

I had a deceased friend who would say, "Big doors swing on small hinges." My best friend, Jesus, who is still living says, "With God all things are possible." Amen (Matthew 19:26)

Ralph's Graduation
Brother Bob, Mom, Dad, sister Brenda in front of
Dad, Ralph, & Ricki

Week of Evangelism

While I was a student at Johnson Bible College, one of the annual traditions was the Week of Evangelism held the week before Easter. All the students worked at different churches.

My roommate was from Martinsville, Virginia and had preached often at a small African American church near his home. He asked me if I would go home with him and preach one night at the church. I said, "Sure."

The first night he preached, and I sang a solo. They did not have a pianist, so I sang acapella. I was doing fine until the congregation decided to join me with their rhythmic version making it a congregational song. I soon became one voice in their congregational choir.

The next night I preached, what an experience! A nice-looking well-dressed gentleman really enjoying the service closed his eyes and kept saying "preach, preach, preach." To a young preacher just starting to learn to preach that was like putting gas on a fire. After the service, my friend said, "You preached about forty minutes."

I certainly was into their style of worship. I have always been blessed when I had the opportunity to preach for our African American brothers and sisters. They know how to encourage you with their "amens, that's right, yes, preach" and many more.

Ramblin' Through Our Story

Ricki Finally Said "Yes"

When I was still in college, I preached at a church in Duhring, West Virginia, outside of Bluefield. Some of us preacher boys drove from Kimberlin Heights, Tennessee each weekend to preach at our weekend ministries.

On a Saturday night I was dating Ricki. I called that "personal evangelism." I wanted it to sound spiritual. I was trying to get her to marry me, but she kept saying, "Ralph I would never marry a preacher." I was striking out that is for sure.

One weekend I asked her to go to Duhring on Sunday with me. We would stay with a family during the day and drive back to Bluefield on Sunday after church. She agreed to go with me.

On the way home she scooted over next to me and said, "Ralph, I've decided to marry you." I said Ricki, "You always told me you wouldn't marry a preacher." She said, "After hearing you preach, you are not enough preacher to matter." If I had been a good preacher, she probably would not have married me. You really did not believe all of this did you? The part about her going to church that Sunday is true. I hope it made you smile.

My "Child" Bride

I graduated from Johnson Bible College on Sunday. Ricki graduated from high school on Wednesday. We got married the following Sunday, June 1, 1958.

We went to the courthouse to get the marriage license. Because Ricki was seventeen her dad had to sign for her to get married. Since I just graduated from college, I had no money, so her daddy not only signed for her but paid ten dollars for the license.

Sometime later I told people I was so in love I could not figure out what was going on. Once my head cleared, I saw "the light." Her daddy was not going to let a signature and ten dollars stand in the way of unloading her on me.

June 1, 1958: Our wedding day

God Always Provides

In 1958 we were newlyweds in our first church in West Virginia. Money was tight with a salary of two hundred dollars a month. Ricki was to host a lady's group at our home with light refreshments. She informed me that morning that I needed to go buy cookies and drinks at the store. I told her I did not have any money. She said, "The Lord will provide." Later that morning a member of the church drove up in front of the house and honked his car horn. Due to his health issue of "black lung" he was unable to attend church for several weeks and wanted to give us something. He handed me a twenty-dollar bill. After thanking him I went into the house and told Ricki.

God was showing us, early in our ministry, that he would provide for us.
This he has done repeatedly.

Do not doubt his promises. Philippians 4:19 "My God shall supply all your needs according to his riches in glory by Christ Jesus."

My First Board Meeting

I was fresh out of college excited about beginning as a fulltime minister of a church. Ready to take on the world. My first elder's meeting was a "bubble buster." The church had three or four elders but never had a meeting. They just prayed and served communion. I found out very quickly why ---they did not get along.

At that time, the coal mines had several men out of work which two of the elders were part of that group. They both had applied for the night watchman job at a local business. They begin discussing that position in the board meeting. During the conversation one elder called the other elder a liar. He replied, "You shouldn't call a fellow Christian a liar, that is harmful to his Christian character." The other elder said, "You don't have any Christian character." I thought to myself, "Lord, this church does not need a preacher, they need 'a referee.'"

Shortly after, the Lord led us to Poplar Springs. They wanted and appreciated a preacher.

More About Dean Clark

Poplar Springs Church had a parttime preacher who was leaving. They were planning to hire a full-time preacher. I had graduated from Johnson Bible College six months earlier and someone had submitted my name for the full-time position. Dean Clark had spoken at Poplar Springs in the past so one of the Elders wrote him a letter (long distance telephone calls were costly at that time) inquiring about me. He responded saying, "If you can get him, get him." Thank you, Dean Clark, for helping me get the full-time position at Poplar Springs Church which I served for forty-five years.

On their travels from Tennessee to Eastern North Carolina to visit their daughter and family Dean and his wife would occasionally come by our house. Dean Clark's first wife passed away and he had remarried. Several years later Dean and his new wife stopped by Poplar Springs one Sunday to worship. The Elder who had written him to inquire about me approached Mr. Clark saying, "You told us how to get Ralph as our minister, can you tell us how to get rid of him?" Thankfully, Dean Clark did not offer any suggestions.

Moving Day to North Carolina

On January 1, 1959, Ricki and I moved to Poplar Springs Church in King, North Carolina. It was a rainy day in Bluefield, West Virginia. We had everything we owned in a pickup truck and our old mint green 1951 Mercury. That was long before the interstate highway that now tunnels through the mountains. We had to cross three two-lane mountainous roads in West Virginia and travel through Fancy Gap Mountain in Virginia. By this time, the rain had turned to sleet. My mother and father came with us to help drive. Oh yes, one more thing, Ricki was pregnant with our daughter Kathy.

When we arrived at the church parsonage located in Rural Hall on old highway 52 in Forsyth County, people from Poplar Springs were there to help us unload. The church was located off highway 66 in Stokes County a few miles away. Little did we know on that day that this was the beginning of a major portion of our lives.

Forty-five glorious years of great memories to be precise.

Early Years at Poplar Springs

When we began our ministry at Poplar Springs, the church attendance was around one hundred twenty-five. The old white framed church building was still standing, the classrooms in the back were being used for Sunday school.

I was the first full time minister. Dennis and Wanda Fulton had been part time at Poplar Springs and King Church of Christ (presently First Christian Church). Being the only minister, I wore many hats – preaching minister, youth minister, worship leader and choir director. Ricki was the church secretary. In our case it was all right for the church secretary to sit on the preacher's lap.

The church I preached at in West Virginia paid us two-hundred dollars a month. This translated into fifty dollars a week for a four Sunday month with forty dollars for a five Sunday month. Poplar Springs paid us sixty-five dollars a week. I jokingly told Ricki that we had "hit the big time" making all that money. I found out differently real soon.

Ralph in the pulpit at Poplar Springs

Poplar Springs – The Growing Years

During our forty-five years at the church, we grew considerably with the love and support of the congregation. We would joke with the congregation that they could not criticize us, because they "raised" us. Ricki was eighteen and I was twenty-three when we came to the church. The church campus grew through six building programs and six land acquisitions. The staff went from one to six full-time and part-time positions. To God be the Glory.

What turned out to be forty-five years were an incredibly happy and rewarding ministry. Early in those years God blessed us with two children: Kathy and Paul.

We retired from Poplar Springs on December 31, 2003. In the next few years, we had two interim ministries in Virginia. Later we went to Surry County and ministered thirteen and one-half years to the lovely people at the Dobson Church of Christ.

As I often tell people, we have lived and are living a blessed life. If we had a choice, we would do it all over again. We have no regrets!

Ricki, the Cook

Ricki, my wife, has distinguished herself as an excellent cook, caterer, and hostess – par excellence. This all happened after we got married and she learned to cook from the good southern cooks in North Carolina. Her ladies Christmas dinners hosted at our home were an annual event to look forward to and be remembered.

Before we married the only thing, she could prepare was spaghetti. It was good, but I did not want to eat it three meals a day. Oh yes, she baked me a devil's food cake for my birthday. Just as Eve tempted Adam in the garden with fruit, Ricki tempted me with chocolate cake. I got in good trouble; we have been married sixty-six years.

Now that we are experiencing the "empty nest" and getting older she does not cook as often. To be truthful if I want to hide anything from her, I put it in the stove. She will never find it there. Ricki is a good sport, but I better stop picking on her.

My Two Speeding Tickets

(I did not say, "My only speeding tickets.")

For many years Poplar Springs Church supported an orphanage in Grundy, Virginia, Grundy Mountain Mission School. One fall Saturday we loaded six cars with several needed items (food, clothing, and other necessities) and headed north to the school for a full day's journey. Since I knew the way, I was the lead car. All the cars had their headlights turned on so we could see to stay together.

When we got into Virginia I took a short cut through a crooked back road to Tazewell, Virginia. After a brief time on this road a little girl in one of the other cars got sick. Two cars stopped, but I was not aware of this fact. Remember it was a very curvy road. Suddenly, I saw a blue light coming up behind us. The highway patrolman said we were speeding. We had to follow him to the jail house in Tazewell. By this time, the two cars that had stopped caught up with us. Here we go, a highway patrolman with his blue light flashing leading six cars up the highway with their headlights on. Other cars on the highway thought we were a funeral procession so they either stopped or pulled off the road to show their respect. If they only knew, we were possibly under arrest and headed to jail. I commented to the people in my car, "I have been in funerals that were not this sad." We did not know what was going to happen. When we got to the jailhouse the first question people asked an officer, "Where is your bathroom?" Four of the six drivers got tickets. On our way home we decided we would place our speeding tickets in the church offering plate on Sunday and tell the treasurer we did not have any money left for the offering that we had to spend what money we had in Tazewell, Virginia at the jailhouse.

On Sunday morning as the men were counting the offering they came upon those pink tickets. Someone asked Leo, one of the drivers and a counter, "Leo, did you get a ticket yesterday?" He said, "yes." They picked up another ticket and asked, "Did Joe get one too?" he said, "Yes, keep going the preacher got one also." We have laughed numerous times about this story; and it is true.

****

Be careful if you go to Washington, North Carolina. I went to speak at the Terri Cia Church of Christ in Pantego, North Carolina which is near Washington, North Carolina. Dr. Davey Stallings and his wife Nancy went with Ricki and me. We stayed with friends. After church, our hosts said, "Let's go to Greenville for lunch. It will be on your way back home." Davey and I were following our host couple Gary and Elaine Respass, along with Nancy and Ricki. I was stopped by a highway patrolman for speeding. My friend called us asking, "Where are you, I can't see you." In a soft voice I said, "I'm getting a ticket." By the way I lost money on that speaking engagement.

Years later in the early part of 2023 my Pantego friend called me to ask if I would come in August to preach a revival making it my 250th revival. I told him I would on two conditions: First, with our age, health issues could prevent us from coming. They needed to have someone to back me up just in case. Second, if I get a speeding ticket he would pay for it. He agreed to the first condition but would not the second. Do you blame him?

My Most Embarrassing Moment

Have you ever had a sigmoidoscopy? I did. If not, you do not know what you have missed. The doctor had me on the examination table on my elbows and knees with me fully exposed. His nurse came into the room to assist him. He is using a metal flexible scope. I am extremely uncomfortable. The nurse wants to talk, I want to agonize. She said, "Aren't you Joe and Jane Brown's (not their real names) preacher?" I wanted to lie, but my preacher's conscience would not let me. So, I grunted out a "uh-huh." She said, "I am their next-door neighbor." I thought, I hope I never see this woman again! I could not be so lucky. Months later I got up to preach and guess who I saw in the congregation seated with Joe and Jane? Yep, my new acquaintance, the nurse, and her husband. It so happened that Joe's mother played the piano for the church services. After the service she hurried down the church aisle to introduce me to her son's neighbors. They both reached me at the door at the same time. When she started to introduce us, I said to her, "She knows me better than you do." The nurse and I laughed. Joe and Jane became members of Poplar Springs Church. Sometime later they moved away.

After Ricki and I retired from Poplar Springs we went to a church in Surry County to do an interim ministry. Guess who was the members of that church? You got it my sigmoid nurse, and her husband. I was their minister again. We had another laugh. We laughed several times about our awkward introduction. It wasn't that funny when it happened.

Friend, you cannot make this stuff up. Life is funnier than fiction!

Don't Get Overconfident

There was a time when one of the most popular songs for funerals was "How Great Thou Art." I was asked to sing this song so often I got comfortable and thought I did not need to have a copy of it when I would sing the song. That was a big mistake. I was asked to sing it at a funeral at Hayworth Miller Funeral Home in Rural Hall. The first verse and chorus went fine, but the second verse was not so good. I forgot the words, so I started making up words. I was so embarrassed but somehow got through it. One of the men from Poplar Springs came up to me and said, "Preacher, you did a good job on your song, but you sang some words I've never heard before." I replied, "You will never hear them again, I don't know what I sang."

Lesson: Do not get too confident, you can embarrass yourself. I know from first-hand experience.

Jimmy, the Carpenter

The church built a new parsonage next to the church and we happily moved into our new home in1964. When the parsonage was built it was not a practice to put rollers on the kitchen cabinet drawers. Over time the drawers became crooked and hard to open and close. Ricki asked Jimmy Holmes if he would come and fix that problem.

I was in India with my friend Dean Davis working two weeks with our friend Aji Lall, a missionary. Because of the time difference, I called home one afternoon, which was morning in North Carolina. A man answered the phone. I thought I must have dialed the wrong number. I asked, "Who is this?" He said, "Jimmy." I did not recognize the voice, so I asked, "Jimmy who?" He said, "Jimmy Holmes." I asked, "What are you doing in my house?" He said, "I'm working on Ricki's drawers." Honestly, all this story is true. Ricki had gone grocery shopping while Jimmy was repairing the cabinet drawers. Of course, the humor is in the play on words.

Domestic Disputes

I have read and heard that one of the most volatile situations a police officer can encounter are domestic disputes. Preachers are not immune from them.

There was a couple, she suffered from emotional instability. They had been quarreling for several days. He called me on Saturday asking me to come to their home and talk to her. When I arrived, she was in their bedroom holding a twenty-two rifle to her throat with her finger at the trigger. Her husband told me the gun was not loaded. In my strongest authoritative voice, I called her name telling her to put the gun down. It worked. She laid it on the bed. I went into the bedroom picking up the gun.... oops the gun was loaded!

At this point she ran into the kitchen, grabbed a knife, and placed it on her neck as if she were going to cut her throat. I took it away from her. Yes, she was committed to the hospital for psychiatric care.

Another experience I had was when a married man took another man's wife to Florida for a week. When they returned home the two couples decided to get together to solve their problems. A family member asked me to come to be a peacemaker. Oh me, I went! As I entered the room I could feel the tension. I was extremely uncomfortable.

They began to talk. The guilty woman told the guilty man and his wife that her husband had been carrying a pistol since they returned from the trip to Florida. The angry husband looked at the guilty husband and said, "I came prepared to take care of you today." My first thought was, "what am I doing here?" My second thought was, "where is the closest door?"

I learned one thing that day: I am not a conflict solver. I am a chicken. I am afraid of getting lead poisoning ---- from flying bullets.

Friends, the ministry is very demanding, but it certainly is not boring.

Ricki and the Ties

There was a tie factory in Pilot Mountain, North Carolina where you could buy expensive quality ties for five dollars each. I would visit it occasionally and buy four or five ties. I came in one day with a few ties to which Ricki said, "Ralph you don't need any more ties you have plenty and furthermore we can't afford them." I said Ricki, "I like pretty women and pretty ties; do you want me to spend money on women or ties?" That was the end of that conversation. It never came up again.

It Is True

You have heard the saying, "It isn't what you know it is who you know." I know this to be true.

Through the acquaintance with Wilmer "Vinegar Bend Mizell", who pitched baseball for the St. Louis Cardinals and became the congressman from our district in North Carolina, Ricki and I, along with another couple received an invitation to the National Prayer Breakfast in Washington, D.C. Richard Nixon was president at this time.

Don East, who was a member of Poplar Springs Church and a senator in the North Carolina Senate invited me to open that chamber in prayer twice.

Both events, the National Prayer Breakfast and attending the North Carolina Senate were special moments.

Memorable Moments

Memorable Baptisms

Baptism is a very important time for a person who is accepting the Lord Jesus as their savior. They are obeying the command of the Lord (Matthew 28:19 & 20). Several baptisms I witnessed have stuck in my memory.

Len White, a special young man, born with cerebral palsy. He was very intelligent and very faithful to attend church. When he decided to give himself to the Lord and be baptized four of his friends carried him in a wooden chair into the baptistery. It was a very moving moment. It was much like the story in Mark 2:1-5 when four men removed the roof from a house to lower their paralyzed friend down into the house to be healed by Jesus. Len's friends brought him to Jesus for spiritual healing.

****

I had the opportunity of baptizing a "big" round chested man one time who was a "floater." After trying numerous times to totally submerse him, I finally got him under enough to complete the baptism. If you think that is funny…try submerging a beach ball!

****

The oldest person I had the opportunity to baptize was sixty-nine years old. When he came up out of the water he said, "I've been under water plenty of times, but it never felt this good before." Naturally, he has just been 'born again'" as Jesus told Nicodemus in John 3:3.

****

When I was preaching a revival in Matoka, West Virginia during the summer of 1955, a sixteen-year-old girl came forward. The next night, she brought her baptismal clothes in a brown paper bag. She was crying. Her younger sister had come with her. They told me their daddy said when they got home, he would spank her if she got baptized. I baptized her and accompanied her home to tell her father. He was not as mean as his threatening talk.

P. S. A few years later I read in the newspaper that her father shot and killed his next-door neighbor. Obviously, he had not changed.

****

Shortly after I graduated from Johnson Bible College, I preached a revival that summer at the country church in Kentucky where Dean Davis was the minister. The church did not have an indoor baptistery. When people came forward to accept Christ, we took them to a creek located up the road. The congregation would drive to the creek and shine their headlights on the baptisms. What wonderful spiritual memories.

The Baptism of John Mitchel

In 1957, I was preaching in Duhring, WV. I had preached a revival there that summer. We baptized on Sunday afternoon in a creek below the church which a train trestle crossed. Before the baptism, a gray-haired gentleman from the church came to me and asked that we sing an invitation (which we did not normally do at baptisms). He said "there is a man here to see his daughter baptized. He has not been to the revival. He is a miner, and he is not a Christian." When we sang the invitation, a man began walking off the train trestle down the bank towards the creek. When he did, I saw the elderly gentleman who asked us to sing the hymn bent over and began to cry. I reasoned that must be the man about whom he was thinking. His name was John Mitchel. John had on a new pair of slacks and shirt (people usually brought their baptismal clothes in a brown paper bag). I asked John if he wanted to go home and get some more clothes. He said, "No, I want to be baptized in these and he was! John never missed a Sunday at church for about a year. Within the year after John was baptized, he was diagnosed with cancer. In the last few days of his life, he was bleeding through cancer spots on his body. His caregivers were changing the sheets every few hours. He died in his own blood at home. Moral– If you have never made your peace with God, do not delay. You never know you could be like John, not long before you meet your maker.

The most important thing to remember is…regardless of where a person is baptized be it an outdoor pond, creek, river, ocean or an indoor baptistery of any size church baptism is where Jesus said one is "born again" (John 3:5). It is where one is buried with Christ (Romans 6:1-6) and becomes like Christ (Galatians 3:27). Also, it is where our sins are forgiven, and God's Holy Spirit comes into us to guide and strengthen us. (Acts 2:38)

Memorable Weddings

Weddings are part of the minister's responsibilities, although they are very time-consuming. I have performed two hundred and six weddings. No matter what amount of time is involved in planning the wedding, sometimes the unexpected happens. Here are a few of my experiences.

One of the North Carolina laws pertaining to marriage at one time required the marriage license to be purchased in the same county the wedding is performed. That law has changed because of cases like this one. We were having a wedding on Saturday at Poplar Springs Church which is in Stokes County. On Friday, the groom came to the parsonage which at that time was in Forsyth County and the county he had purchased the marriage license. He wanted to know what to do. I called the register of deeds and was told, "It happens all the time." The office said to have the couple go through the vows in Forsyth County, fill out the documents then go to the church in Stokes County for the formal wedding. On Saturday morning the couple came to the parsonage in regular clothes, the bride with hair curlers with Ricki as a witness and they left legally married.

At 2:00 pm we went to the church for the public ceremony. The photographer was following us around, so the groom said to him, "Why don't you go and get pictures of all the pretty bridesmaids instead of us. He replied, "I want to take a picture of you looking at the marriage license." The groom looked him in the eyes and said, "I'm already married." I had never seen a more puzzled look on a person's face, as if he were asking, what are we all here for? After we explained what happened, we all had a big laugh. None of the wedding audience realized they were part of a mock wedding.

****

A wrestling match after the wedding....

On one occasion the wedding I performed was to be at two different locations: the church at one and the reception at another. While I was in my office at church preparing the necessary paperwork on the marriage certificate I heard a terrible noise in the hallway. When I opened the door, I saw three big boys in tuxes going at it---two against one. It was the groom and two groomsmen. I said, "guys you are going to tear those tuxes." They said, "that's alright we'll pay for them." The groom had played a trick on one of them at their wedding and now it was "payback time."

When the groom and bride finally ran out to the car to leave, those guys had taken a chain with a lock and cowbell and locked it around his waist. It was comical as he ran with the ringing cowbell. The groom told me later, they had to stop along the way to get bolt cutters to cut the bell off. They will not forget that---neither will I.

****

Wrong ring wedding...

At one of my weddings when I ask the maid of honor for the groom's ring, she gave me a ring with a pink stone that obviously was a lady's ring. My first thought was I had been given the bride's ring. My second thought was in these crazy changing times maybe that's what they are doing these days. I went on and gave it to the bride and she put it on the groom's finger. After the wedding, the maid of honor said to me, "I guess you wondered what was going on when I gave you the ring." I said, "Yes, I was." She said I was in the bathroom and in a hurry. I laid the groom's ring on the counter rushing out I left it. Knowing I had left the ring when it was time to give you his ring, I took one of my rings and gave it to you." That cleared up that confusing matter.

Memorable Funerals

Out of more than seven hundred and forty-five funerals I have been a part of in seventy years of ministry there are a few that stand out because of the unusual circumstances.

I conducted a funeral of a man who did not attend church, very few people were present. I preached, sang, read scripture, and prayed. The funeral home was short of help, so I even drove the flower truck to the grave site. The only things I did not do were embalm the body and dig the grave. Friends, the ministry is full of surprises.

I performed the funeral of a young man who was a C.B. (citizen band) buff. This was before cell phones. He would talk on the C.B until early morning. He died unexpectedly one night while he was talking on the C.B. When he was buried, the family, knowing his love of talking on the C.B., placed a C.B. mic in his hand.

Another funeral of distinction was an elderly lady who always wore her apron and carried her snuff can in her hand. So, to make her look natural in the casket her family honored her by burying her in an apron with a snuff can in her hand.

These funerals made me think, what if we had a custom to bury a person with what was most important to them by placing it in their hand. What would be placed in your hands? Your Bible, a picture of Jesus, or your family? Or would it be an empty beer can, a cocktail glass, a marijuana joint, your cell phone to access porn, maybe cash money or your last financial portfolio statement. Only you can answer that question.

Ramblin' Through Family Stories

My Family

Ralph (myself) and Rita (Ricki, my wife)
Our Children– Kathy and Paul
Kathy's Family– Husband Mike (deceased)
Daughters– Sarah and Hannah
Sarah's Family– Husband Matt
Sons– Abram and Ezra
Hannah's Family – Husband Joe
Sons– Roman and Micah
Daughter– Evie
Paul's Family
Son– Jonathan and Daughter– Elizabeth
Jonathan's Family– Wife Natalia
Son– Leo

Ricki, Kathy, Ralph, & Paul

A Young Baptism

When Kathy was around 4 years old and Paul was about two years old, they had a small inflatable wading pool in the back yard. Just as I walked out the back door, I saw Paul in his little "speedo" trunks grabbing the side of the pool trying to get out of the water. I asked them what they were doing, and Kathy said, "I just baptized Paul." That is the youngest baptism by immersion I ever heard of.

They Learn Early

After church one Sunday we were invited to a family's house for lunch. After the meal, the adults retired to the living room to visit. Paul and Kathy were outside playing with the other children. While playing they had come upon a dead bird and decided to perform a funeral. I asked them how that went. I was informed Paul preached and the other children sang. We asked what did you sing? They said, "Happy Birthday to You." I guess if that is the only song you know, it will work for a bird's funeral.

Out of the Mouth of Babes

When our granddaughter Sarah was small and playing outside, she ran inside to get her mother, Kathy, to go outside with her. Sarah wanted her mom to see the sun rays filtering through the clouds. Obviously, Sarah was very impressed by something. She said, "Mommy you know what that is? I think someone has died and Jesus is opening the door to heaven to let them in."

Jesus said, "Anyone who will not receive the Kingdom of God like a little child will never enter it." (Luke 18:17)

Don't Always Tell It All!

When our son Paul was around four years old, I had outpatient surgery to remove a cyst from the end of my spine. The doctor also removed a cyst from my scalp at the same time. When I came home Paul wanted to see my bandages. Knowing how inquisitive and indiscreet he could be, I only showed him the one on my head.

Because of the spinal surgery I was unable to sit down for a few days. I laid on the bed or the sofa. A few of our church members came by to check on me. Of course, Paul would give them the medical explanation showing them the bandage on my head. He told them "Daddy had a knot removed from his head and he can't sit down." Now you know why I did not tell or show him the one surgery causing the most pain.

They Do Listen

When Sarah, our granddaughter, was around eight years old I preached a sermon on "Integrity." The sermon content covered the subject of honesty. After church Mike, our son-in-law and Kathy, my daughter, took their family to a local restaurant for lunch. A lady had left her purse where they were seated. Sarah took the purse to the front reception area and turned it in. The lady, discovering she had left her purse, returned to the restaurant to get it, hoping someone had discovered it. The receptionist told the lady what had happened and pointed out the little girl and her family who were leaving the parking lot. The lady followed the car and when they stopped, she thanked Sarah for being so honest, giving her a $10.00 reward.

As soon as Sarah got home, she called us saying, "Papaw, you know the sermon you preached this morning on being honest?" I said, "Yes." She told me what had just happened. She felt good about herself.

There is an old proverb that says, "What you learn in the Holy Place should be practiced in the marketplace." Sarah did!

Concerning integrity and honesty. People go through life concerned about their image and reputation. They should be paying attention to their character. Your character and integrity should be as straight as the Empire State Building and as solid as the Rock of Gibraltar. If you take care of your character your reputation and image will take care of themselves.

Ricki Never Said Anything

On one of my speaking engagements at Mid-Atlantic Christian College (formerly Roanoke Bible College) this one time I will not forget. It was the school's Annual Gospel Rally. Before I started to preach, I told a few humorous stories; some on Ricki (you do know humor is the shortest distance between two people).

After the service Ricki told me there was a couple sitting behind her having a conversation concerning me. The guy said to the lady, "That man is crazy." Ricki said, "I wanted to turn around and say, 'that is my husband'." I never decided why she did not say something. Did she not want to embarrass them, or did she not want to acknowledge her husband was crazy?

Better Left Unsaid

We got Ricki a used Jeep Grand Cherokee. I told her it has all kinds of "bells and whistles." When I turn the key in the ignition your name comes up on the dash. She said, "No it doesn't." I said, "Look there is your name 'Airbag'." I shouldn't have said that! I did not see her for three days. Around that time, I finally could see her just a little bit out of my left eye. Part of this is true. I'll let you decide which part.

An Unforgettable Day

Our granddaughter Sarah is married to Matt Splawn. They have two lovely boys, Abram and Ezra. In the middle of a work week, she was having back pain and asked me to take her to the emergency room at Novant Hospital. After a few hours of assessing the doctor informed us that Sarah had cancer. That was an unexpected "punch in the gut." This was one of those times when I was trying to be strong for her as she was trying to do the same for me. We were in a state of complete disbelief.

She has been through countless chemo treatments, scans and all that goes along with this dreaded disease. During all this, Sarah has been a role model of courage and inspiration to numerous people. She is now the administrative assistant at Poplar Springs Christian Church. She and Matt are leaders of the teen group. She pushes herself to do far more than is expected, although her sickness and treatments deplete her of the energy needed. She recently re-baptized two of her lady friends. Sarah is the proverbial "energizer bunny." Please pray for her and her family. The Lord needs ambassadors like her to testify to his name and power.

We Got Towed

Mack, a close friend, had season tickets to Wake Forest University basketball games. One Wednesday night Wake was playing their archrival, North Carolina Tarheels at 9:00 pm. He gave me the tickets. My daughter Kathy and I decided to go after church, arriving as the game was about to start. The coliseum parking lot was full as well as the parking lots of local businesses who were closed for the evening. We were frantically looking for parking space at this point when we spotted a few empty spaces at "The Peek-A-Boo Club." As I pulled in Kathy said, "See that sign? The sign read "Violators car will be towed off." Not wanting to miss the game I said, "They can't tow all of us off." We parked, saw the game which Wake lost. It was starting to rain when we got to the parking lot and guess what, our car was gone. The tow truck was still hauling cars off. Someone was able to find out the towed cars were in Walkertown. It would cost us $100.00 to get our car. Kathy said, "Daddy, I don't have $100.00." Thankfully, I had just got paid so I had the money. Our car had to be gotten out by midnight or wait until the next morning…time was running out.

We called Mike at home who had fallen asleep on the couch, so Hannah answered the phone. Hannah woke him up and told him he needed to go get us because the car had been towed. He thought he was dreaming, so he went back to sleep. Finally, Hannah was able to wake him. We got to the parking garage just in time.

I told the story to a few people just for laughs. A few weeks later one of them had a certificate from The Peek-A-Boo Club printed for me which was placed on the pulpit that Sunday. The certificate stated I had a lifetime membership with free parking to the club. I saw it and laughed. By then I had to tell the whole congregation the story. What a laugh that received. The disappointing news is I have a lifetime membership to The Peek-A-Boo Club, but they have gone out of business.

It Really Happened

When Ricki and I had been at Poplar Springs twenty-five years, the church surprised us with two new cars. Saying we were surprised is an understatement, we were totally shocked! We just concluded our annual Christmas program. As the norm the church was packed. Everybody but Ricki and I knew what was going on. After the closing prayer Ricki and I were walking down the aisle to speak to people as they left. One of our elders, Richard Westmoreland, said, "Wait a minute I want to say something." He called us back up front, made some kind remarks about our twenty-five years of service and pulled out a set of car keys. He said there is a car parked out front for you. It was a Nissan Maxima. What a surprise!! He then reached in his other pocket and said, "I found another set of keys to a car for you Ricki." It was a Buick LeSabre. That was too much, overwhelming, and humbling. They had put spotlights on the church roof shining down on the two cars in the church yard. Needless to say, we did not sleep much that night. What a memorable and unforgettable event.

Mike's Death

Our son-in-law, Mike Jessup passed away January 2023 at Wake Forest Baptist Hospital surrounded by his loved ones. Hannah, his youngest daughter, was standing close to him. As his breaths got further apart, she begins whispering in his ear, "Daddy you are almost there. Daddy you are almost there." She "spoke" him right into the presence of the Lord. It was a very moving experience. That evening the family gathered in the dining room of our home discussing and reliving the day. Sarah, Mike's oldest daughter, and Hannah openly expressed their deep personal faith in the Lord. It was truly a "God Moment." I will never forget that Spirit led occasion. We all were so blessed by each other's faith at a time when we needed it.

You Grow Spiritually Through Your Valleys

Our granddaughter, Hannah, was fourteen and a half years old when she had a health episode at school. She fainted while sitting at her desk. After being revived and seen by a medical specialist it was discovered she had an issue with her heart and needed a pacemaker.

Her pacemaker has been replaced three times. Each replacement has improved over the last. She now is married to Joe Yoon with three children, Roman, Evie, and Micah. Amid burdens there are blessings.

Our son Paul was recently diagnosed with multiple myeloma. This was another shocker. He is receiving treatments. With all of these and other family tests two thoughts keep coming to my mind. One, the old proverb, "All sunshine and no rain makes a desert." Two, I Peter 5:7 KJV, "Casting all your cares upon him; for he cares for you." Our spiritual growth really does come in our valleys more than our mountains. Do not forget…bad things do happen to good people.

Ramblin' with Preachers

Finding Your Purpose

1950 through 1953 my high school years were struggling years for me. You rarely find the right direction or the right road without a struggle. Listen, young people in high school and college let the Lord lead you in the right direction, that means putting Him first and He will direct you to the right road.

I had graduated from high school and was still searching for my purpose and direction in life. Not knowing at that time God was working.

In 1954 when I entered Johnson Bible College, I wanted one thing, to be a preacher. When you attended JBC at that time you went for one of two reasons: to be a preacher or missionary. Churches did not have youth ministers, music leaders, or associate ministers. The budgets in most churches did not allow these positions.

When I was hired by Poplar Springs Church January 1, 1959, I was the preacher, youth minister, choir director and worship leader. Ricki was the church secretary, which consisted of preparing the Sunday bulletin. With all these responsibilities we also were new parents. You talk about wearing a lot of hats! It was overwhelming! Today I am eighty-eight years old and still only aspire to be one thing---A PREACHER!!!

I was ordained into the ministry on June 23, 1957, about a year before I graduated from Johnson Bible College (now known as Johnson University). My ordination was conducted at Calfee Memorial Christian Church in Bluefield, West Virginia. I do not recall all the details of the service, but I do remember the charge I was given. The charge from II Timothy 4:2, Apostle Paul was speaking to his young successor Timothy, "Preach the word; be instant in season, out of season." What do these words mean? There will be times when people will be eager to hear the word of the Lord and there will times when they will turn a deaf ear to God's word. But Paul encouraged young Timothy to preach God's word when it is acceptable and when it is unacceptable. I have lived to see both times. The way Christianity is being attacked today in our predominantly secular culture, "preaching the Word" would be "out of season."

I recall when I first started in the ministry, revivals were very popular and well attended. This was before the age of "mega churches." All the churches I was acquainted with were rural or in small towns and communities. Friends, that was when preaching was "in season." Today preaching God's word is "out of season." Today we are not worshiping at the altar of the Lord we are worshiping at the altars of materialism, education, narcissism, etc. All these false idols have eroded the moral foundation of Judeo-Christian faith and our country. Remember one of the "top ten", "You shall have no other God before me." (Exodus 20:3 KJV) What I preach today may not be politically correct nor is it in season, but it is "The Word." I was charged to preach, even when it is out of season. Preaching should always be scripturally based. Jesus said, "Heaven and earth will pass away, but my words will never pass away." (Matthew 24:35 NIV). Our message is not temporal but eternal.

****

John 1:14 (NIV)

Speaking of Jesus the scripture reads, "We have seen his glory, the glory of the one and only who came from the Father, full of grace and truth." Since the message we preach is Jesus Christ the Son of God our preaching should also be full of grace and truth.

Ralph's Ordination on June 23, 1959,
at Calfee Memorial Christian Church
in Bluefield, West Virginia

My Personal Thoughts on Preaching

Preaching is the most important responsibility a minister has. While within a week, you may be called upon to comfort a family dealing with death; or visit the hospital room of someone sick; or perhaps some spiritual counseling falls with your duties, etc. But you will have more influence over more people on Sunday morning than any other time of the week. You need to be at your best, prepared spiritually and mentally. Quoting the words of Samuel as God was calling him under the guidance of the prophet Eli. The audience is saying to you on Sunday morning, "Speak, Lord your servant is listening." (I Samuel 3:10)

As a spokesperson for God, you were not called to perform weddings, conduct funerals, fill the baptistery, set up tables and chairs, etc. All of which fall under a minister's job duties. You were called to preach! Give it your best!!!

A Different Generation

Revivals were big in my generation. They were the most evangelistic event of the year. Many people accepted the Lord at them. They were special.

Around 1954 before air conditioning, I led singing at a revival in a small rural church outside Bluefield, West Virginia. Revivals were usually conducted in the summer. All windows were open, which of course allowed the bugs to enjoy whomever they wished. The attending folk used hand-held fans advertising for the local funeral home. Since there was not enough seating inside the small church, people stood outside to hear the singing and preaching. Those days are probably over.

Reverse Astronauts

We live in a very selfish, self-centered, narcissistic culture. People think they are the only person who matters. I refer to them as "Reverse Astronauts." An astronaut is a person who revolves around the world; a reverse astronaut is a person who thinks the world revolves around them.

Jesus told a parable about a highly successful farmer who looked at his fields ready to be harvested, but his barns were already full. After he pondered on what he should do, he decided to tear down his small barns and build larger ones to store the harvest. Eleven times in that story the farmer mentioned "I, Me, My or Mine." You can read the entire parable in Luke 12:16-21. He was a reverse astronaut. Does that describe who you are? I hope not.

Biblical Preaching is Still Important

The church should be the conscience of the community, the voice of God in the community. If the church endorses the values of our secular culture, such as the killing of innocent unborn children created in the image of God or, embrace same sex marriage or encouraging changing their sex which God gave them at birth, the church has lost its influence in the community. It is no longer the voice of God in a dark and dying world. The church should be like John the Baptist of whom the Prophet Isaiah said, "The voice of one crying in the wilderness 'prepare ye the way of the Lord.'" (Matthew 3:3)

Preaching on biblical morality in the average church in America today is like firing a shotgun into a crowd. A lot of people are going to get hit. This is why so much of what you hear from the pulpit avoids biblical morality.

We have tried to dignify sin by giving it new names. People living together unmarried is not referred to as adultery, it is cohabitating; taking the life of an unborn child is not called murder it is abortion; homosexuality is called an alternate lifestyle.

May I politely remind you that Jesus did not suffer his horrific death on the cross for cohabitating, abortion, or alternate lifestyles. He suffered pain and public humiliation for <u>sin</u>. Do not be ashamed to call disobedience to God what His word calls it…it is sin! We try to complicate what our Lord made so clear and simple.

Jesus faced these same issues in His day, and He dealt with them with compassion and love. So can we. Read John 4:1-12 - Jesus

and the woman at the well and John 8:1-11 -
the adulterous woman.

Paul's admonition in Ephesians 4:15 is
wise counsel, "Speak the truth in love." Try
it, it works. Sometimes attitude overshadows
the truth.

Preacher Isaiah Moore

Isaiah Moore was a short bald headed
African American preacher who lived in
Kentucky. He was an interesting individual.
He would get to preaching so fast he would
stop, raise his hand, and say, "Hold on Spirit
don't lead me so fast."

I heard him tell the story about how he
became a preacher. He was a small child
playing on the floor of his family's house as
his mother was dying. His older siblings were
trying, without success, to get him to be quiet.
His mother told them it was all right that
Isaiah did not understand the situation. She
said, "Bring Isaiah to me." She held him in
her arms and prayed for him to be a preacher.
He said, "I would go through fire to preach."
What a testimony!

Wayne Smith

"Bob Hope" of the Christian Church

Wayne was the well-known and much-loved minister of the Southland Christian Church in Lexington, Kentucky. He was called "the Bob Hope of the Christian Church" because of his great sense of humor. He also had a reputation for being very generous.

One year when we attended the North American Christian Convention, we saw one another at the vendor's booth that sold cassette tapes of the convention sessions. The more tapes you would buy the cheaper the price per tape. Wayne told me to get the number of tapes I wanted, and he would do the same and he would pay for them, and I could repay him. Good idea, Wayne. He paid the vendor with a hundred-dollar bill saying, "thank God for funerals."

Poplar Springs Church asked Wayne to speak several times: at a revival, family retreat and banquet.

After his retirement we asked him to speak at a banquet at the church. I went to

Greensboro Airport to get him. As we were walking through the airport I asked him, "Wayne, how do you like retirement?" He set down his briefcase raised his hands, in praise, and said, "Hallelujah, no more weddings." I understood his feelings.

You can see one of the reasons Wayne was loved, he made you laugh.

Proverbs 17:22 (NIV) says, "A cheerful heart is good medicine." What does that mean? A loose interpretation is: If you laughed more, you may not need to take as much medicine.

"Touché"

We had a gifted preacher to preach a revival at Poplar Springs who happened to be short to which I can identify. Not long afterwards at a youth convention in Tennessee I introduced Glen VanMeter, who is six feet plus in height and from Poplar Springs to a preacher friend from Kentucky. He also was the height of the evangelist and me. Big tall Glen looked down at me condescendingly and asked, "Ralph, are all preachers short?" I said, "No, Glen, just the good ones."

****

When people ask me if I have preached any since I retired, I tell them, "Some, when I do it is baseball preaching." They ask, "What is that?" I reply, "Hit and run." That usually gets a chuckle.

Isaiah 6:1-8

Here are thoughts about one of my favorite Old Testament scriptures Isaiah 6:1-8. Isaiah had a life changing experience the year King Uzziah died. He saw the Lord in all his majestic splendor and realized how important a holy life is and how much God wants his people to be holy so he can use them for his glory and praise.

Of all of God's attributes, and they are many, his holiness apparently excels them all. The flying angels (Seraphs) were not saying, "love, grace or power." They threepeated for emphasis, "holy, holy, holy is the Lord Almighty the whole earth is full of his glory."

We read this again in Revelation 4:8 by the four living creatures. The scriptures often remind us to be holy.

The scripture says, "Be holy because I am Holy." We should take this seriously. We serve a <u>holy</u> God who indwells us with His <u>Holy</u> Spirit who saved us through the <u>holy</u> birth (virgin born) of his <u>holy</u> Son (who was sinless). We need to pay attention to our lives and actions.

Because of childhood influences in my life, I was led to believe that holiness meant women were not to cut their hair, wear make-up and must wear long dresses. After further study of scripture, I got a clearer biblical understanding of what holiness means. The Holy Spirit enters our life at baptism (Acts 2:38) and empowers us to live a holy life which goes beyond one's physical appearance. He influences our decisions, conduct and everyday demeanor.

Friends, man's problem is not that he cannot be holy but through the one who is in us, the Holy Spirit, he can. (I John 4:4) Man's problem is he does not want to be holy.

"But you are a chosen people, a royal priesthood, a holy nation. A people belonging to God, that you may declare the praises of him who called you out of the darkness into his wonderful light." (I Peter 2:9 NIV)

Holy living is a prerequisite to entering the presence of our Holy Lord in his eternal home. "Who shall ascend into the hill of the Lord? Or who shall stand in his holy place? He that hath clean hands, and a pure heart; who hath not lifted up his soul unto vanity, nor sworn deceitfully." (Psalm 24:3-4 KJV)

Preaching

A well-known preacher once said, "It takes three things to be a successful preacher: the mind of a scholar, the heart of a child, and the hide of a rhinoceros." I am not the sharpest knife in the drawer, nor do I have the mind of a scholar, but I do have the heart of a child and the hide of a rhinoceros. As I heard said, "Two out of three ain't bad!"

Preaching is like throwing Jell-O against a wall. Most of it slides off but some of it will stick. When someone comes up to me and says, "I will never forget what you said in one of your sermons......" or some years later someone says, "Your sermon on

..........in that revival was what led me to be baptized, or you inspired me to be a minister." That is when you realize that some of it stuck, and it is the pieces that stick that keep you "preaching the Word."

On June 13, 2023, I was picking up food at a local restaurant. Two ladies were standing there. One of them asked, "Are you Ralph Sproles?" I said, "Yes." She proceeded to tell me that her aunt speaks of me often, and they are the Eastman's from High Point. Our mother was the camp nurse at Camp on the Mountain. She then called her aunt, and we facetimed. Her aunt said, "I have wanted to thank you for a long time to tell you how much I was blessed by your camp classes. You were a big influence on me." (Note: this was sixty years ago.) I asked, "Where are you now?" She answered, "In Texas." The wonders of modern technology.

Do not forget I Corinthians 15:18 "Your labors are never in vain in the Lord." Ecclesiastes 11:1 "Cast your bread upon the waters, for after many days you will find it again." Remember I said, "Some of it sticks."

They Said It, You Think About It…

Which "Gang" Do You Belong To?

The second revival I preached was in the summer of 1955 in Montcalm, West Virginia. One night twin brothers ages nine or ten came forward to accept the Lord. I knew how some people thought back then that a person under twelve years of age (that was when Jesus went to Temple and got separated from his parents, Mary and Joseph) didn't understand what they were doing. Knowing this, I asked them, "Boys, what does this decision mean to you?" One boy in typical youthful language said, "It means we have to quit the devil's gang and join the Lord's gang." You cannot say it any better than that!

I have seen people through the years who didn't know which "gang" they belonged to. You see them in church on Sunday and think they belong to the Lord's gang, but you observe them the rest of the week, listen to their foul language, dirty jokes, watch them drink their adult beverages; see them watching porn on the internet, witness their dishonesty and say to yourself, "I don't know which gang they belong to.

Where Are You Going?

There was a lady who attended Poplar Springs Church, whose husband never came with her to church. One Sunday as she went out the door, she said she wanted me to visit her husband. She informed me that he had been drinking for two weeks. The following week I went to see them. They lived in a small mobile home. She introduced me to her husband. I sat down in the den area. Her husband walked into the kitchen, reaching into the cabinet over the stove getting a whiskey bottle. He finished drinking what was left in the bottle. The wife said, "Can't you leave that stuff alone while the preacher is here?"

He came into the den and began telling me about the places where he had worked and the type of work he had done. He said he had once worked on Capitol Hill in Washington, DC. He told me he knew Sam Rayburn, who was Speaker of the House from Texas. Then he said, "Preacher I have always said 'it is not where you have been that matters but where you are going.'" A truer statement has never been spoken! Those true words did not come from the mouth of a preacher, but from the lips of a drunk!

Just remember, it does not matter where you have been, who you know, or how much you have that matters but where you are going? Think about it!!

Elderly Wisdom

The first church I served in West Virginia, while I was still in college, had an elderly gentleman in his late eighties or early nineties attending. He could not hear well, but never missed church. One Sunday a young man asked him why he kept coming to church when he could not hear the sermon, the prayers, announcements, or the singing. He said, "I want everyone to know whose side I'm on."

Friend, stop making excuses for not going to church----your example is important.

****

Some Lessons We Learn Too Late

There was a man at Poplar Springs who in his early life had no time for God or church. He spent his time chasing money. He had three children, but he never took his family to church.

When he got older, he started attending church, was baptized, and was concerned about his grown children and their unchurched families. He tried to talk to them about the Lord and the church, but he had lost his influence over them, and they were not interested.

He and his wife invited Ricki and me to their home for lunch one Sunday. He and I were in the living room talking. With tears in his eyes, he told me about his children's reaction to his conversation with them about the Lord and church. Then he said, "Preacher if I had been as interested in the Lord and church as I was in making money, I would be better off today." Some lessons in life we learn too late.

Gleanings to Ponder

Is it okay to mark in your Bible? The answer is yes, but it is more important that your Bible mark you.

****

It is never wrong to do what is right!

****

If you see a Bible that is falling apart, it probably belongs to a person who is not.

****

When I go to church, I do more than just visit. So, when they finally roll me in, God does not ask, "Who is it?"

****

A person wrapped up in himself makes a mighty small package.

****

People do not care how much you know until they know how much you care.

****

Jesus' slogan could have been, "you catch them, I will clean them.

"Yea, though I walk through the valley of the shadow of death." (Psalm 23:2 KJV) Where is death? Just the other side of the next heartbeat. We live in the "valley of the shadow of death 24/7."

****

We have misplaced values in this materialistic world: houses, cars, etc. God does not care about the size of your house. He cares about the person in the house. He does not care about your expensive car. He cares about the person in the car. Get your values from heaven not earth!

****

Read II Corinthians 4:16 and 5:1-9. We are not in the land of the living going to the land of the dying. We are in the land of the dying going to the land of the living.

Two Special Mission Trips...

Australia

I had the opportunity to go to Echuca, Australia to preach for a week. I stayed in the home of a church family who had four school age children. Australians drink hot tea. I introduced them to American southern iced tea. They loved it. Every afternoon after school they wanted iced tea.

I learned one of their customs that was interesting. The first service for the revival was on Sunday morning. When the service was over everyone would sit for about five minutes quietly before leaving. You have heard the saying, "when in Rome do as the Romans do." Not knowing why, I sat down and remained quiet. After church I asked the preacher why. He said they sit quietly to think about what was preached in the sermon. I liked that! The attendees did this after each service that I preached.

We Americans start visiting, going home or rush out to eat. We lose the spirit of the service and soon forget the spiritual message which we need. The Australian custom is not a bad idea. Think about it.

India

My friend, Dean Davis, and I went to India to work with missionaries Ajai and Indu Lall for two weeks. What an amazing, enlightening, and unforgettable experience for me.

Two experiences stand out in my mind. We spent two days in Delhi before going to Damoh where the Lall's lived and did their mission work. The second day, Dean and I went to the lobby of the hotel for breakfast. The hotel clerk was standing behind a large marble counter with a beautiful ornate mirror and a small brass idol. As he finished his act of worship, he took the idol and placed it in a drawer. He then proceeded to help us. My initial reaction was how sad it is to worship a manufactured god so small that it fit into a desk drawer when our God covers the entire world. Later I began to think that is not much different than what some Americans do in worship. They take Jesus out of their figurative closet for Sunday worship. But when they get home, they place him back in the closet. He is not with them throughout the week. He is not with them at work, during their social life, their free time, or their recreational life. He has little or no effect upon their daily lives, how sad.

Remember Jesus' words, "Why do you call me Lord, Lord and not do what I tell you." (Luke 6:46 (NIV) If Jesus is not Lord of all, He is not Lord at all. If Jesus is not your Lord all the time, he will not be your Lord some of the time.

The second experience while we were in India, we received a phone call that a local government representative wanted to talk with us the next day. They wanted to know the reason foreigners were visiting their country. We were a little nervous.

The individual who questioned us could not speak English and we could not speak Hindi. So Ajai Lall interpreted for us---Good! He asked questions which Ajai interpreted, and we would reply. In turn Ajai would give the government agent our answers. I am not sure we gave the correct answers, but Ajai gave the answer the agent wanted to hear. It must have satisfied him because he left, and we were not arrested. This reminded me of a passage of scripture. Romans 8:26 – "In the same way, the Spirit helps us in our weakness. We do not know what we ought to pray for, but the Spirit himself intercedes for us with groans that words cannot express." Thank God for His interceding Spirit.

I Saw Three Kings

In 1967, I was blessed to go on a thirty-five-day trip to the Bible lands in the Middle East with a group of twelve. What an amazing trip that enabled the Bible to come alive to me in many ways.

One of the most unique experiences we had was to see three actual kings. We called that being at the right place at the right time. The first king we saw was in Cairo, Egypt. After dinner one evening as we were walking down the street, we noticed several limousines lined up at the hotel across the street. We asked someone what was happening and were told, "The King is coming." In a short time, a large man with his Arab headdress and long robe got into one of the limos. He was the King from Saudi Arabia who had been dethroned by his half-brother and was exiled in Egypt.

A few days later we were in Jerusalem Jordan, just before the six-day war that summer. Jerusalem was a divided city at that time. Traffic had stopped and we asked our driver what was the hold up? He said, "The King is coming." We swiftly jumped out of the car running to see the young King Hussein of Jordan as his motorcade left the Parliament building where he had been the speaker.

We were in Athens, Greece when we saw a large group gathering. Among them were U. S. sailors from the Sixth Fleet. We asked why the crowd? You guessed it. The answer was the king is coming. Shortly a young handsome man got out of a small helicopter that had landed and got into a small sports car. He was King Constantine of Greece. That was an exciting experience for a mountain boy from West Virginia.

Let me tell you it does not begin to compare to what is ahead for us. One of these days there will be a trumpet sound heard around the world. People will ask, "What is that?" They will hear, "The King is coming! Not just a king but 'The King of Kings.'" I hope you are ready!

Think About It?

What is a sacrifice? A sacrifice is to give up something you want for something you want more. (Romans 12:1 KJV) "I beseech you therefore, brethren, by the mercies of God, that ye present your bodies a living sacrifice, holy, acceptable unto God, which is your reasonable service. And be not conformed to this world: but be ye transformed by the renewing of your mind, that ye may prove what is that good, and acceptable, and perfect, will of God".

God loved his virgin born son dearly. (Matthew 3:17) He was willing for his son to die for something He wanted more ---to restore fellowship with His most loved of all creation, humankind, you and me, which was lost in the Garden of Eden because of the sin of Adam and Eve. (Genesis 3:1-24) Read the "golden text of the Bible." John 3:16 (NIV)

"For God so loved the world that he gave his one and only son that whoever believes in him should not perish but have eternal life." Have you sacrificed anything for the Lord? He sacrificed something (his Son) for you.

Just Ramblin'

Ohio Revival

One of the best revivals I had the privilege to preach was with Pat Mooney in Sebring, Ohio in 1981 with Shan leading the worship. Pat would provide Shan and me with the names of prospects to visit as he would be visiting prospects also. It was thrilling to have people coming forward every evening.

Years later Pat and I were recalling the meeting and he told me his wife got pregnant that week with one of their children. I said to him, "You rascal, while Shan and I were out making visits, you were home making babies." Naturally, we had a big laugh.

Ricki and GPS

Ricki and I were on a trip that required us to use the GPS to get to our destination. We stopped to eat. After getting back into the car and starting it, the GPS kept repeating "recalculating, recalculating." At the same time, Ricki had decided to play a Christian music cd. Frustrated with the GPS she said, "I wish that lady would shut up so I can listen to my cd." I said back to her, "Now you know how I feel." We did get a laugh that we both needed. Ricki is a good woman to put up with me.

Go Get "Sally"

I preached a revival in Kentucky. During that revival we had lunch with a family who lived in an old two-story white frame house. As well as I can remember the meal was good until the man of the house asked his wife to "go get Sally." I was waiting for her to bring a family member who was living with them and needed help because of being in a wheelchair or using a walker or cane. Much to my surprise she brought a black plastic box and placed it on the table. That was "Sally." Sally was the ashes of an elderly lady whom he had befriended, helping her with chores and other necessities. She wanted him to have her remains. So, Sally joined us for the remainder of the meal but didn't eat or say anything -- Ha! Ha! To say the least this was an unusual but delightful memory.

About Being Short

I have always been teased about my height or the lack of it. My stock reply has been, "It isn't the size of the dog in the fight but the size of the fight in the dog." When I was in high school my next-door neighbor encouraged me to apply for a job as a "bagboy" where he worked as a butcher, Acme Super Market. The manager told my friend because of my size I would be unable to carry two big grocery bags to the customer's car. Naturally, I was disappointed. One Saturday the store was extremely busy and needed more bag boys. The manager asked my friend to call me to help. I went and I hustled, bagging groceries, and carrying them out. I got hired! When I left to go to college, I had attained the manager's position of the produce department. Remember, "It is the size of the fight in the dog."

****

When Ricki and I were planning to leave the church in Duhring, West Virginia, a friend told me of a church in Kentucky that needed a preacher. I preached a trial sermon at that church Sunday morning and then traveled to Poplar Springs Church on Wednesday to preach another trial sermon. As Paul Harvey would say, "Now you know the rest of the story." Poplar Springs hired us, and we stayed forty-five glorious years. But here is really the rest of the story. It was a few years later that my friend in Kentucky told me why the church there did not call me… "I was too short!" That is one time being short was a blessing.

****

Often when I stand up in a seated crowd someone will yell, "Stand up Ralph." Everybody will laugh, including me. It is healthy to laugh at yourself.

****

One time I was asked to speak. When I got to the pulpit someone had placed a stool for me to stand on. Even my preacher friends could be cruel. One preacher asks me why I was short I replied, "My mother was short, my daddy was short, I guess it is hereditary." He said, "I read in the Bible, why you are short." I said, "I didn't know the Bible said anything about it." His reply was, "The Bible says, the wicked shall be cut off." No Respect! There is more....

One night in Bible study I was teaching on Zacchaeus, the little fellow who climbed a tree so he could see Jesus. One man in the class spoke up and ask the class, "Do you know what Zacchaeus' last name was?" We all said "no." He said, "It was Sproles." All the times I had read that story, I missed seeing that.

Of all the comments about my being short, there is only one time it hurt. When we first came to Poplar Springs in 1959, the preacher's office was in the parsonage located on old highway 52. Naturally, I was at home in the mornings working. Kathy, our daughter, was about three or four years old. She had noticed I did not leave in the mornings and come home in the afternoons like the other men in our neighborhood, so she did not think I had a job. One day she and I were riding down the road she asked,

"Daddy when you get big are you going to work?" It is a little upsetting when your own child notices you are short.

It Never Worked for Me!

In 1995, Jimmy Walker had been recently elected Mayor of King, North Carolina. He was traveling to the outer banks of NC for a governing conference. On the way he was stopped for speeding. After the officer saw his driver's license, he said, "I see you are from King." Jimmy said, "Yes sir." The officer said, "Do you know Ralph Sproles." Again, he politely replied, "Yes sir." The state trooper told him he had heard me speak at a rally. The trooper said, "I'm not going to give you a ticket, slow down." Jimmy told me that story sometime later. I said to Jimmy, "I know Ralph Sproles better than you know Ralph Sproles, but my name never got me out of any speeding tickets."

My Best Prank

Olin, a very gifted preacher had preached in Kentucky for several years. His wife had passed away and he was living in Florida. Atlanta Christian College in Atlanta, Georgia asked him to come to Atlanta to teach a class. While in Atlanta he was spending time with a widow he had met. During this time, he also had reconnected with a widowed college mate who lived in Indiana.

Poplar Springs had invited Olin to preach a revival at the church. Every night after the service he would call the widow in Indiana talking for an hour. His Indiana friend was aware of the Georgia lady. He told the Indiana friend she had bought a new Cadillac car. She told him, "If he wanted a Cadillac, she would buy him one."

After the revival he was flying to Indiana to see his lady friend. When I came home from the office Ricki told me Olin had left his under shirt and shorts in the bathroom after his shower. I told her I would take care of them. I packaged them up and mailed them to Indiana to his friend's house with the return address "Cadillac Lady, Atlanta, Georgia." She laughed at it, Olin did not. He told me later, "If I could have got my hands on you, I would have choked you." As one well known comedian would say, "the devil made me do it."

My One Claim to Sports Fame

By flying with US Air on previous trips, I had accumulated two free trips to anywhere in the United States. I tried to get Ricki to fly to California with me, she said, "No." She was afraid to fly. So, I asked my son and my son-in-law if they wanted to pay for one ticket between them and fly to Arizona to play golf on desert courses. They agreed to. We got five other friends and took off to Phoenix, Arizona. On the second day, we played the TPC Course in Scottsdale. I was playing with three of the guys. Let me remind you I am not a good golfer, but occasionally I do get lucky. This was one of those days. I hit a good shot- just like the pros – and it rolled right in the hole. The biggest difference was I hit with a five wood, while the pros would use a pitching wedge.

Two of my partners had already hit their shots and were sitting in their cart waiting for us. My other partner was on the tee behind me. I heard him exclaim, "I've never seen that before!" He just stood there with a stunned expression on his face.

When we got back to the club house one of them told the pro about the hole in one. He walked me into his office and begin asking me all kinds of questions: "What kind of ball were you playing, what brand of clubs were you using, what kind of shoes were you wearing?" And several more. My son said, "Daddy, they asked everything else, did they ask what kind of underwear you had on?" I said, "No, but if they had I would have told them 'Messed up Hanes.'"

Just in case you are interested, my name is still on a brass plate on the wall at the clubhouse. If you ever visit the clubhouse at the TPC Golf Course in Scottsdale, Arizona, check it out!

My Beer Invitation

One beautiful fall day Mack White and I were going to a Wake Forest football game.

We were walking through a group of tailgaters, and one hollered out, "Do you want a beer?" I shouted back, "No, thank you." Mack said to me, "Ralph that is the first time I ever heard you turn down a beer." I said to Mack, "It is also the first time you ever heard me offered one, isn't it?"

You Explain This One

A member of Poplar Springs Church who had passed away was originally from Mt. Airy, NC. His funeral was held at a funeral home in Mt. Airy. The associate minister, youth minister and I conducted the service.

He was to be buried in a church cemetery near the Blue Ridge Parkway in Virginia. It was an extremely cold winter day with a strong wind. The little church sat on a ridge. You can imagine how cold it was. I do not have to tell you the committal service was very brief.

As we all hurried back to our cars, a young fellow from that area ran by us and said, "It is colder than a mother-in-law's love." We laughed. I had never heard that expression before or since. If he meant "it was bone chilling cold," I agree with him. We still laugh about it.

Wrong Shoes

John, a friend, invited me to go golfing with him and some of his friends. I enthusiastically accepted. It happened that we had identical golf shoe bags with the same new brown and white shoes, which we would be wearing for the first time. What are the chances of that?! My friend kept complaining that his feet were hurting, and his shoes were too tight. Although I never said anything, I also thought, "My shoes were looser than when I tried them on at the golf shop." After nine holes of hurting feet, John decided to change into his regular shoes to finish the remaining nine holes. At the end of the golf game while putting our clubs away and changing our shoes the mystery of the shoe problem was solved. We realized that we were wearing the other's shoes. John wore size nine while I wore size seven---poor

John! That story floated around King for quite a while.

While we are talking about golf, here is one more. A few people have asked me, "Preacher, have you used foul language on the golf course?" I tell them, "No, but sometimes where I spit the grass dies." I have killed a lot of grass playing golf.

Pay the Bill

One Friday evening Ricki and I with Dr. Davy Stallings and his wife, Nancy, our very dear friends, went to a restaurant in Kernersville, NC where they had never visited before. Usually when the bill is presented either he or I will say, "I'll get the bill." So, tonight he volunteered. As we were leaving, our wives decided to utilize the facilities. The restaurant was crowded, and people were waiting to get seated. With all this commotion we neglected one necessary thing.

On Saturday afternoon Dr. Stallings called to say that he and Nancy had gone back to the restaurant that morning for breakfast. I said, "You must have really liked the restaurant." He said, "We did, but I forgot to pay last night, so I went back to eat and pay last night's bill."

I still kid him that I must watch him, or he will get us arrested. It is healthy to laugh together!

Bus Trips

One of the most enjoyable experiences Ricki and I had during our ministry at Poplar Springs was going on bus trips with members and friends of the church. We made ten or twelve trips as far south as Charleston, South Carolina, east to the Outer Banks of North Carolina and north to Canada. Wayne Hauser from King, North Carolina was always our safe, dependable driver. We made so many new friends.

Each day we began with scripture, prayer and singing. Of course, I told a few jokes. We created a lot of laughter and memorable moments that we continue to reminisce about today. Our days were full of riding, sightseeing, programs, and plenty of eating on and off the bus. People still come up to me and say, "I wish we could make another bus trip." I tell them, "I have aged out. I could not keep up with what we did on those trips." I am getting tired just writing and thinking about all those special times with God's people.

No Hotdog Monday

On a beautiful September Monday Ricki and I decided to take a ride to John Brown's store to get a hotdog for lunch. We think their hotdogs are one of the best in King. When we get there, we found out they are closed on Monday... no hotdog.

Our saliva glands are still wanting a hotdog. So, we take off to Pullium's in Winston-Salem, about a thirty-minute drive. A place well known for their hotdogs. When we get there, yep you guessed it, they are also closed on Mondays. Disappointed, we started the trek back home still wanting a hotdog. Then we remembered a place called The Red Caboose, known for their hotdogs, on old highway 52 which was in the direction we were going. Not only was it closed but had changed its name to Cowboy Train. Still no hotdog.

Driving towards home we went by Cook Out, again hoping for a hot dog any hotdog. As we were coming up to the diner there was a sign on the billboard that read "Special Cook Out Hotdog." Boy, our mouths were watering at this point. We were ready to pull in when we saw the place was closed. Another disappointment. After driving twenty miles and one hour, still no hotdog. The moral of this true tale is…If you are in the King area on a Monday and want a hotdog, go to the Dairio.

About the Author

Ralph Sproles graduated from Johnson Bible College (Johnson University) in 1958 with a BA. He served a short time in various churches during his college days and shortly after graduating. In 1959 he was called to Poplar Springs Church of Christ in King, North Carolina, where he served for forty-five years. Although he retired in 2003, he continued to preach when asked. He served thirteen and one-half years at the Dobson Church of Christ in Dobson, North Carolina retiring in 2022. He is still preaching when called upon and loves every minute of it. This book gives details of his many years of serving our Lord. He wants this book to be informative, entertaining, inspirational, and humorous.

www.ingramcontent.com/pod-product-compliance
Lightning Source LLC
LaVergne TN
LVHW051248080426
835513LV00016B/1803